The
Buffett Strategy

$854,000
not $220,000

The Simple Way to
Beat Wall Street Professionals

Law Steeple MBA
Warren Buffett's Investment Strategy:
Set It and Forget It

IAN Books

An IAN Books paperback

Published by
IAN Books
41 Watchung Plaza, B242
Montclair, NJ 07042

Copyright © 2017 IAN Books

All rights reserved. No part of this book or its Interactive Internet CD can be reproduced, transmitted in any form or by any means, electronic or mechanical, including photocopying, recording, or by any information storage and retrieval system, without the written permission of the publisher.

Cover photo: Warren Buffett KU Mark Hirschey

Special sales for education use by nonprofits:
IANBooksEditor@yahoo.com

ISBN-13: 978-1978481022

ISBN-10: 1978481020

IAN Books at Amazon.com

Wealth Without Wall Street:
Buy Direct -- Avoid the Commissions, Fees, Loads

The Insiders' Guides to Buying Discount Financial Services:
Buy Direct and Save $3,000 Every Year

Drop Your Insurance:
Buy Only What You Need

Create Financial Freedom Using Your Wealth Reserve ™:
Fix your financial life

The Simple Financial Life:
How to get what you want without going into debt and living paycheck to paycheck

Build Wealth Without Extra Money or Time:
You don't need to budget or get an extra job

Tax-FREE Retirement:
Use the tax code for lifetime income free of tax

The Working Millionaire:
$2,000,000 Tax-FREE Wealth Reserve ™ Self-insure Self-fund

Build Your Own $2,000,000 Tax-FREE Wealth Reserve ™:
Self-insure Self-fund your lifestyle

Stop wasting $3,000 every year:
101
financial products ***NOT*** to buy and why

Long-term Care Insurance:
Is it right for you? Are there better alternatives?

Contents

Simple Low-Cost Investing Beats Wall Street	5
1. Avoid income taxes.	8
2. Buffett's investment plan.	11
3. Compound stock earnings.	13
4. Buy buy buy investing.	16
5. Avoid high-fee managers.	18
6. 'I can beat the market.'	19
7. Invest every month automatically.	22
8. Buy low-cost financial products.	24
9. Manage investments once a year.	26
10. Plan spending wisely.	27
Use the *Buffett Strategy* to reach your goals	29
The Author	31

Simple Low-Cost Investing Beats Wall Street

Warren Buffett has proved it, again. You do not need Wall Street 'professionals' to reach your financial goals. In fact, if you use them, you may give up <u>63%</u> of your potential accumulations because of trading, charges, commissions and fees.

Buffett made a bet with a hedge fund manager for $1 million 10 years ago. So far <u>Buffett's strategy has earned over 7% a year versus 2.2%</u> for Wall Street's best and brightest.

Buffett has advocated a simple low-cost strategy for decades: Buy the stock market index in a fund like Vanguard's 500 Index. <u>Invest in the market returns</u> consistently and you will do better than everyone you know. Instead of $854,000 at $250 a month you end up with $220,000 because of Wall Street costs. Over the long term, your returns would average over 11% per year. *DALBAR* keeps track of returns and found that the <u>average managed-account equity investor earned just 3.79% a year</u> over 30 years ended 2014. The benchmark returned 11.06%.

We buy the stock market index at the <u>low cost of 0.04% and so earn 11% over time</u>. We avoid the 'load' or commission, the poor-timing trades and <u>hidden charges</u>: purchase, redemption, 12b-1 fees. We don't need an advisor to decide to buy or own this fund. In fact, they take fees whether we receive a benefit or not. And don't be fooled by 'no-commission' ETF: Expenses near 1% a year.

Also note, since 1997 we have been able to invest for the long term without paying ANY taxes on the gains. In the past, we had to pay for gains in our 401k, IRA and pensions in retirement. We can avoid the charges to start and maintain these tax-advantaged accounts too. Earnings are FREE after age 59 ½. That can mean $99,000 produces $901,000 tax-FREE income!

With large mutual fund firms like Vanguard, we can do all this with one hour's phone call or web session. We do NOT pick stocks or time the market with our contributions. No system has been proven better than automatic monthly contributions. We can have them transferred automatically to the trustee of our account.

Warren Buffett has shown us that success is about allowing

our money to work in the market *over time*. The important part is 'over time' since Wall Street makes its money by promising to beat the benchmark. There is only one money manager who has come close: Warren Buffett. His record is 20% a year since 1965.

The real secret to investing is **compounding**. Buffett says:

"My wealth has come from a combination of living in America, some lucky genes, and **compound interest**."

You can earn $1,000,000 with $250 a month over time with 11% or just $208,000 with advisor average of 3.79%. Your choice.

Compounding is earning money on the money you already earned last period. Look at the account returns on page 14. This client earned $3 million by investing $123,000 over 41 years in the equivalent of a stock market index account. He averaged 11.77% from 1962-2003. There is no other investment that has been that consistent.

No one can tell what will happen in the future so you must rely on what we know now not what some Wall Streeter claims will happen to your money in the future. Remember, you pay them whether you reach your goals or not. You take all the risk while they have none. And no refunds.

So it is either the Buffett Strategy or your advisor's ideas. People who owned the market benchmark since 1976 have earned about 11%. An advisor's charges reduce the amount you get to keep. If they charge only when they earned your goal, fees would be fair. However, that is not what happens even some of the time.

We can chose to invest in a fund that gives us the stock market average of 10-12% or we can go with a Wall Street professional's research and hunches and market timing. Beware that despite the occasional 'killing' you hear about in the press, very few clients *actually* receive earnings that beat the market. An advisor that takes your money for promises of success is not unbiased. Since Warren Buffett does not profit from promising us a bright future, let's take *his* advice.

Warren Buffett, the greatest investor of our time, says to use low-cost funds that match the market. Playing the market by trading stocks and timing the market gyrations is the loser's game. No one including Buffett knows what will happen in the future. In other words, the probabilities of earning 11% from a large group of profit-making companies around the world is greater than the very *remote* chance that your salesperson can pick the next Apple.

We beat Wall Street by using Warren Buffett's strategy: buy and keep buying the largest mutual funds run at cost and owned by us, the investors. We can't afford hedge funds, offshore tax shelters, and expensive Wall Street money managers taking 2-3% a year. Most can't beat indexes anyway. Buffett won the bet after 10 years.

A plain market index fund beat 92-95% of the returns of "professional" managers, including hedge funds. Stock picking by geniuses works for a short time only. We avoid paying Wall Street owners the $1.3 Trillion per year revenues they take from their clients. If you want advice, pay a fee-only advisor for their time like a lawyer.

Why should you give up your advisor? The average return for managed accounts is 3.79%. A low-cost index fund provides 11%. You are giving up 63% of your total potential earnings. Do you really think an expert at selling knows anything about what will happen to a security or market in the next hour, week or year?

Low-cost stock mutual funds are our only viable low-risk asset over time. Other assets have lower or more volatile returns. Anyone with at least 10 years before they need the money needs "purchasing power" and this is especially important for investors under age 65.

It is a tragedy that high-schoolers are not being taught this simple method of investing: The Power of Compounding. If they were shown the chart on page 12 they would understand. Unfortunately, they have not been taught to invest for the long-term. Perhaps Wall Street lobbyists have pressured our professional educators to maintain the status quo.

The ***Buffett Strategy*** uses the only proven method of gaining your first million dollar account:

The **miracle of compounding** is all you need.

Pay $99,000 ($250 month); Return $1,000,000

Avoid income taxes

Part of the Wall Street herd bias is trading which produces taxes for you, not for your advisor. One of the strategies of the wealthy is to avoid taxes on their accumulations. Consider these examples: Buffett pays just 17% **total** tax: http://www.youtube.com/watch?v=Cu5B-2LoC4s; Mitt Romney only **14%**; John Kerry only **13%** and Apple just **9.8%**. Most of the top 1% ers pay far less than the average citizen of this country in terms of disposable income.

If the average family earns $50-75,000, they pay about 14% federal, 13% SS/Med/UC/Health, 10% state/local, 4% sales/excise, or over 30% total taxes. As Buffett said, "I pay 17.7% total tax. My office staff pays 32.9%." Of course this does not include pension and other insurance costs most us also pay.

This is why the wealthy avoid taxes with their businesses and various tax-advantaged vehicles. Trump payed $0. In order to become and stay wealthy, people need to have money to invest. The average family has little extra money to build wealth let alone have enough for retirement. They need tax-FREE compounding.

The following graph makes clear that in order to accumulate $1,000,000 from monthly contributions, we must buy and hold the securities of growing companies worldwide AND pay **zero** tax on the growth to *maximize compounding*. We can see clearly that investing in growing company stocks is more likely to get us to our goal in our lifetime than investing in government bonds or a bank savings account or our advisor's current hot idea.

As your investments grow—especially mutual funds that pay dividends and gains each year—you will not have to pay tax on them because of your special IRS-approved account. Most regular IRAs and pension accounts are tax-DEFERRED *not* tax-FREE. Taxes have to be paid sometime ... except ....

Our special account is a Roth IRA. It allows us to leverage tax-FREE accumulations over time against an immediate tax deduction as with a regular IRA or 401k pension. The benefits can be enormous. For instance, if you make contributions of $250 a month, $3,000 a year to your low-cost stock mutual funds, you could spend $30,000 tax-FREE for every $3,000 you deposited!

Invest $250 a month, $3000 a year, never pay tax

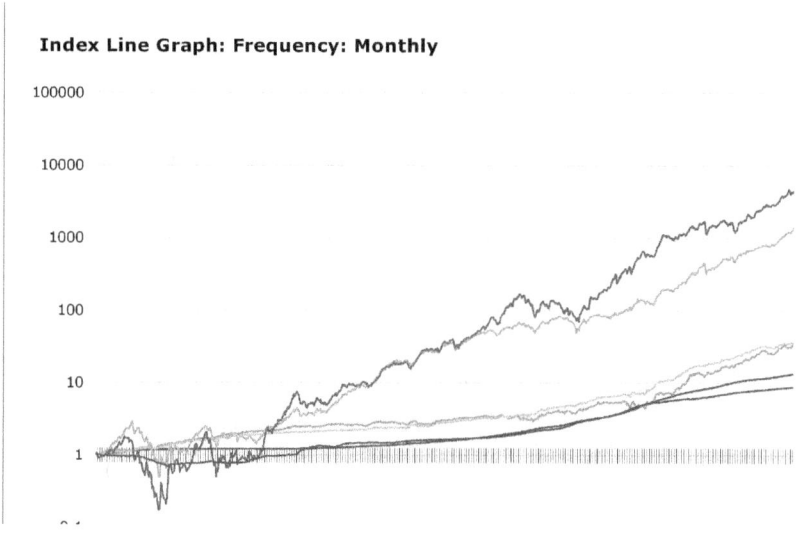

Top line—Small Cap Stocks
2nd line—Large Cap Stocks (S&P 500)
3rd line—US Long-term Corporate Bonds
4th line—Intermediate-term Government Bonds
5th line—US 30 day Government T-bills
6th line—US inflation
Courtesy: Dr. Campbell R. Harvey http://www.duke.edu/~charvey/

Tax-FREE v Taxable

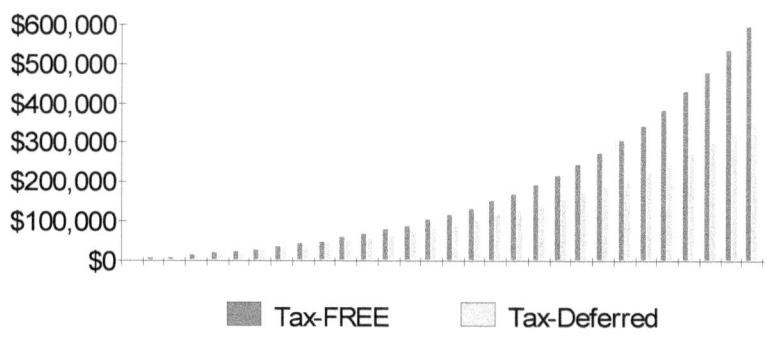

The Roth IRA Rules

Contributions:

$5,500 ($6,500 over age 50) each year
Income under $132,000 (2017) single
married $194,000 (2017)

Distributions:

Tax-FREE for contributions.
And Tax-FREE for earnings if
Over age 59 1/2,
Account open 5 years,
Taxable earnings unless
Disabled,
First home ($10,000),
Death

Bonus:

Account can grow tax-FREE for life
Minimum distribution rules don't apply
Heirs don't pay income tax
Account has no maximum

Check with your tax preparer
https://www.irs.gov/pub/irs-pdf/p590a.pdf

Buffett's investment plan

The rules for the use of your Roth IRA account are manageable by you. You don't need an advisor. The rules are found at https://www.irs.gov/retirement-plans/roth-iras. Your account trustee can answer most questions. You don't need to pay an attorney. All of the large low-cost mutual funds firms are trustees. I will discuss the best firms available below.

You can start this account with any of the firms with no upfront charges. Some charge an annual fee for the bookkeeping. We will consider the specific investment options later. We will use low-cost firms because you will keep more of your own money. You don't need to pay Wall Street to maintain this account.

It is important to pick a trustee with the least costs since over time the annual costs can really destroy your accumulations. For instance, if you use a brokerage firm, you pay 2-3% each year on your balance. You could give up 63% of your earnings. If both spouses have a low-cost account with contributions of $250 a month for 27 years, they could accumulate $1,000,000. If they use a high-cost broker/advisor, both accounts may hit only $282,000. Depending on earnings of 8-10% and total costs of 2-3% per year, you could really hurt yourself. You need to watch the costs. Advisors do NOT beat the markets over the long term. Just stick with your Buffett investment plan.

You can open your account at any age as long as you have *earned* income. Stock dividends or interest do not count. Any job will do. You don't even need a job requiring a W-2 to prove it. A part-time, weekend or night job will do. Any cash-only work will qualify—even for a child. I think accountants recommend that receipts and records be maintained. You could even work for yourself in a home-office business like many rich do.

Nontaxable distributions from a Roth IRA won't affect your eligibility for student aid either. Later, in retirement, this money won't affect your social security benefits as of the rules today.

The ***Miracle of Compounding*** works.

Actual client Tom's account, investing $250 a month, 1962-2003

24%	3,720
16%	7,795
12%	12,091
-10%	13,582
24%	20,561
11%	26,153
-8%	26,821
4%	31,013
14%	38,775
19%	49,713
-14%	45,333
-26%	35,766
37%	53,110
24%	69,576
-8%	66,770
6%	73,956
18%	90,809
32%	123,827
-5%	120,486
22%	150,653
21%	185,920
6%	200,255
32%	268,297
19%	322,843
5%	342,135
17%	403,808
32%	536,987
-3%	523,787
31%	690,091
8%	748,538
10%	826,692
2%	846,286
38%	1,172,015
23%	1,445,268
33%	1,926,197
28%	2,469,372
21%	2,991,570
-9%	2,725,059
-12%	2,403,420
-22%	1,874,601
29%	2,412,905

Compound stock earnings

Compounding high earnings is your *best* strategy. The wealthy get richer just by leaving their money invested. They don't work more hours or take more risks. The famous 1% at the top of society take down 23.5% of all income (up from 8.9% 30 years ago). They don't work any harder than you do—*their money does*.

Because of compounding, many millionaires have said, "the first million was the hardest." It takes a working business person about 34 years to grow $250 a month to $1,000,000 using tax-advantaged investments. However, it only takes 7-9 years to double their money to $2 million. Investors in stock funds, earning 10-12% on average, can double it again to $4 million in less than 10 years without adding new money. Their tax-advantaged accounts make it easier to reach their goal. It is compounding that makes it happen—not Wall Street trading/timing.

Compounding of high earnings means that we make money on our last period's accumulations. The progression looks like the client's account values on the previous page. Notice that our balance can double in a couple of good years. This happens because we are not just adding $3,000 per year, but adding up to 38% of the previous year's accumulation to our balance. We are making money on top of our money with no extra effort on our part. During this 40 year period, this client lost money some years. In fact, they lost 14% and then 26% back to back, but then made 37% and 24%.

Wealthy people don't panic. They have learned that compounding over the long-term is the only way they can build wealth. There are no successful get-rich-quick schemes. To reach their goal, they know there will be setbacks. No business grows steadily upward all the time. They have seen the losses before and they don't sell their assets in a panic.

We will buy assets that "grow by themselves." We will have security because our **_purchasing power_** will grow over time. We begin with a fund with 500 large company stocks. We earn 10-12% and then buy all ten Vanguard funds over time reducing our risk of owning just one fund. When one fund is down, others are up.

The Vanguard Top Ten

2016 Total Return	Fund	Long-term Return	Longevity
11.9%	500 Index	10.9%*	since 1976
33.1%	Energy	10.9%	since 1984
16.1%	Extended Market	10.7%	since 1987
-9.0%	Health	16.4%	since 1984
1.7%	International Growth	10.0%	since 1981
10.7%	PRIMECAP	13.4%	since 1984
18.3%	Small Cap Index	10.7%	since 1960
8.1%	Wellesley Income	9.9%	since 1970
12.5%	Windsor	11.3%	since 1958
13.4%	Windsor II	10.7%	since 1985
11.7%	Average	11.5%	

*Average Annual Returns as of 12/31/16.

This kind of security comes from our regular contributions ... and patience. The ***miracle of compounding*** works its magic on our Roth IRA account when we give it TIME. The wealthy give their money time to compound. They don't take it out and they try not to pay tax every year on the gains. They maintain their contribution schedule because each $100 added is worth $10,000 to them later. They use the compound interest calculator so they know the future value: moneychimp.com/calculator/compound_interest_calculator.htm.

Most people who become wealthy have to wait for years of slow growth in their account. It took client Tom 21 years to get to $150,000. Then it only took 14 years to get to a $1,172,015. After only 4 years, it became $3,000,000. Shortly thereafter he "lost" over a million dollars! Last year his account hit $5 million.

This client stuck with it and was successful in reaching his goal but there are many who do not. Most people who are not wealthy already, have a hard time believing it can happen with only their patience. They just don't have the experience of how compounding works to keep faith in its outcome eventually.

Once an account becomes sizable, we don't need to add contributions to it. Usually, by the time we stop regular employment, we aren't making contributions. Some wealthy people continue to work after age 65 because they love what they do and want to continue. Obviously, they don't need to work but the **miracle of compounding** continues to work.

The annual returns of growing companies

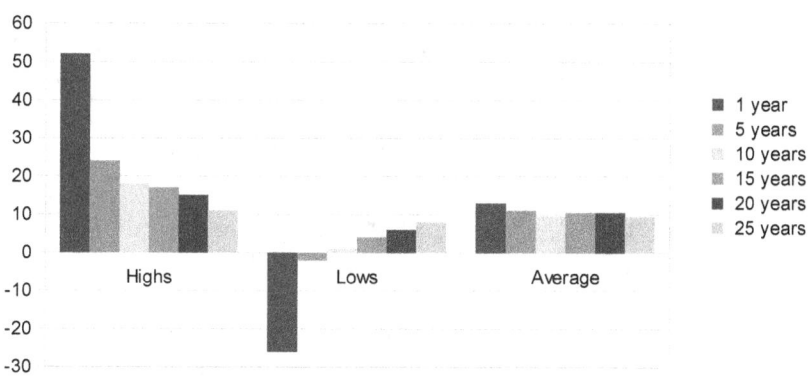
Range of annual returns of stocks, 1950 – 2000

Buy buy buy investing

When we develop the ***habit*** of investing, we take our emotions out of the process. We, as a silent partner must learn to live with the market downs. We need to think of this account as our stake in growing businesses as they rise and fall in value. See page 17.

It is easier to be patient if we make contributions automatic. Like the Social Security contributions we make every payday, the contributions are made automatically. We can have the Roth IRA trustee debit our checking account every month.

As one client told me, "I never see the debits, so I never miss it." Of course this client has already identified the $250 he has committed to his $1,000,000 future. He took my advice and went through his spending on financial services. He used our ***Guides*** to find the $250 a month he was wasting on products and services he would never use or need. In my amazon.com/Insiders-Guides-Discount-Financial-Services/ you will find "**tricks of the trade**" that we insiders use to buy directly from quality manufacturers.

It's easy to say **I will start later**. Starting 5 years later means ending up with HALF the amount we were shooting for. It is hard to believe that missing that $250 a month for 5 years or $15,000 can reduce our total from $600,000 to $300,000.

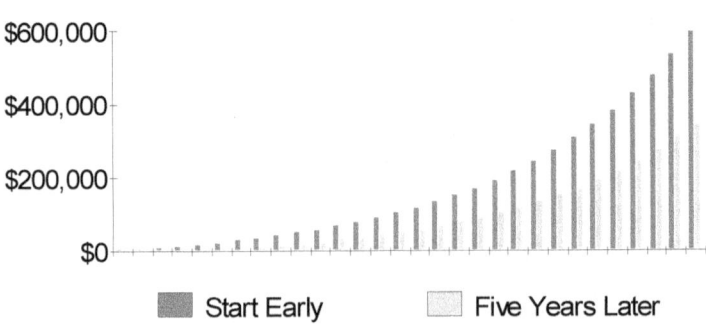

Your investment plan over time

$2,000 Annual Stock Market Investment 1950- '70- '80- '90- 2013

Year	Returns	Balance	Balance	Balance	Balance
		$2,000			
1950	31%	$2,620			
1951	24%	$5,729			
1952	18%	$9,120			
1953	-1%	$11,009			
1954	52%	$19,773			
1955	31%	$28,523			
1956	5%	$32,049			
1957	-11%	$30,304			
1958	43%	$46,194			
1959	12%	$53,978			
1960	1%	$56,538			
1961	26%	$73,757			
1962	-8%	$69,697			
1963	24%	$88,904			
1964	16%	$105,449			
1965	12%	$120,342			
1966	-10%	$110,108			
1967	24%	$139,014			
1968	11%	$156,526			
1969	-8%	$145,844	2,000		
1970	4%	$153,757	2,080		
1971	14%	$177,563	4,651		
1972	19%	$213,681	7,915		
1973	-14%	$185,485	8,527		
1974	-26%	$138,739	7,790		
1975	37%	$192,813	13,412		
1976	24%	$241,568	19,111		
1977	-8%	$224,082	19,422		
1978	6%	$239,647	22,707		
1979	18%	$285,144	29,155	2,000	
1980	32%	$379,030	41,124	2,640	
1981	-5%	$361,978	40,968	4,408	
1982	22%	$444,053	52,421	7,818	
1983	21%	$539,724	65,850	11,879	
1984	6%	$574,228	71,921	14,712	
1985	32%	$760,621	97,575	22,060	
1986	19%	$907,519	118,494	28,632	
1987	5%	$954,995	126,519	32,163	
1988	17%	$1,119,684	150,367	39,971	
1989	32%	$1,480,623	201,125	55,402	2,000
1990	-3%	$1,438,144	197,031	55,680	1,940
1991	31%	$1,886,589	260,731	75,560	5,161
1992	8%	$2,039,676	283,749	83,765	7,734
1993	10%	$2,245,843	314,324	94,342	10,708
1994	2%	$2,292,800	322,651	98,268	12,962
1995	38%	$3,166,824	448,018	138,370	20,647
1996	23%	$3,897,654	553,522	172,656	27,856
1997	33%	$5,186,540	738,844	232,292	39,709
1998	28%	$6,641,331	948,281	299,894	53,387
1999	21%	$8,038,430	1,149,839	365,291	67,019
2000	-9%	$7,316,791	1,048,174	334,235	62,807
2001	-12%	$6,447,855	925,203	296,223	57,095
2002	-22%	$5,024,437	722,291	232,316	46,035
2003	29%	$6,459,474	930,787	301,119	61,730
2004	11%	$7,164,483	1,034,274	336,099	70,664
2005	5%	$7,512,677	1,084,540	352,433	74,098
2006	15%	$8,694,884	1,259,259	412,409	90,450
2007	5%	$9,163,538	1,327,133	434,638	95,325
2008	-39%	$5,601,431	813,388	268,074	60,754
2009	27%	$7,116,358	952,155	342,993	79,699
2010	15%	$8,186,112	1,097,278	396,742	93,954
2011	2%	$8,347,378	1,118,894	404,558	95,805
2012	16%	$9,666,264	1,295,679	468,478	110,942
2013	32%	$12,759,468	1,710,296	618,390	146,443
Avg.	12%	12%	11%	13%	11%

IAN, LLC © 2014   1/2/14   TheInsidersGuides.com   10

Ibbotson Associates **Stocks average 11.4% per year, bonds 5%, CDs 3%.** Stocks have gone up as much as 54% and as low as –43% in 1 year, up to 28% or down to –12% in 5 years, up 20% or down 0% in 10 years, up 18% or up 3% in 20 years. Short term bonds have gone up 14% or up 0% in 1 year, up 11% or up 0% in 5 years, up 9% or up 0% in 10 years, up 10% or up 1% in 20 years.

Avoid "high-fee managers"

"In every single time period and data point tested,
low-cost funds beat high-cost **funds."**

According to an unbiased Morningstar study, low-cost funds beat high-cost funds PERIOD. However, the myth of Wall Street is that you must pay more for good performance. Warren Buffett's mentor, Benjamin Graham, advised to: "buy financial products like we buy "groceries, ... not perfume." You do NOT get what you pay for.

The best predictor of your investing and wealth building success is **low cost**. When we subtract the costs of buying and maintaining investments, we give up a lot of the gains. A stock fund that reflects the overall market is called an index fund. This kind of fund costs only 0.04% ($4 per $10,000). Our account will compound at 10-12% over time.

The chart below makes it clear. Over time, the costs we pay each year will cut our total accumulation by up to 63%. Instead of compounding at 10-12% annually on average, some people give up 1.5-3% of the earnings on their money to the middle person. They end up with less.

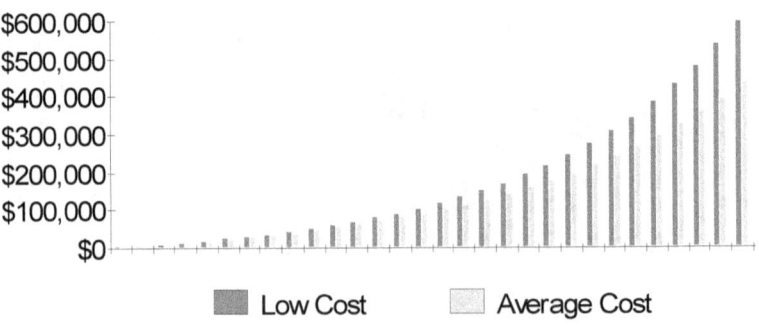

Low-cost index funds beat 95% of funds with a stock-picking manager. Wall Street takes $ 1.3 Trillion of our money in fees.

'I can beat the market'

When your advisor or money manager makes a claim about the future, they are lying. When retail customers don't know how and where to invest properly, sales people make up stories. They don't lie exactly; they mislead. Sales people only survive if they <u>separate you from your money</u> or your potential earnings. You need a plan to accumulate for the long term that takes only one hour to follow.

    Picking ***individual*** stocks as a strategy is not likely to work for us. Professional managers and day traders have had limited success <u>over time</u>. Our strategy is to build wealth as a silent partner in growing global companies. Since it is unlikely that we (or anyone else) will be able to pick the next Google or Apple, we invest in a large group of firms. We do not need to fear picking the wrong one or picking one at the wrong time. We own them all: <u>Apple, Amazon etc</u>. As John Bogle says: "Don't look for the needle. Buy the haystack." This is a proven successful strategy.

    A mutual fund manager advertises that their fund or ETF has "beaten" the market and so we pay 1.5-3% of our assets every year. Over time we find that while the stock market index rose **11.06%,** we earned only **3.79%** annually. In this way, costs can take 63% of our returns over time. Each time they sell and buy, we give up some of our compound earnings. We may incur taxes too.

    When young investors begin investing, they cannot buy all 10 Vanguard funds listed above at once with $250 per month. Vanguard has minimums on all funds so they can keep their expenses low for everyone.

    There are two ways to start our Roth IRA account. The easiest way is to save $250 a month in our savings account until we have the $1,000 minimum for Vanguard's entry fund: STAR #56. We can open the Roth IRA by phone or <u>online</u>: <u>STAR</u> minimum is $1,000. Most Vanguard funds need $3,000 to start. We can keep contributing to the STAR fund until we have $3,000 for the 500 Index and then $3,000 for the Extended Market funds and eventually all 10 funds. Vanguard is at 800.551.8631.

    The second way to begin is to open a Roth IRA at TIAA, the world's largest pension company, primarily for educational and research institutions. Low expenses and low initial contributions make TIAA an organization we can stay with. TIAA 800.842.2888.

At TIAA we can make application and begin immediately with an automatic monthly contribution of $100 or more from our bank account. We can follow how the assets grow by themselves. TIAA has two funds that provide us with the diversity of companies worldwide: TIAA Equity Index and TIAA International Equity.

Request a prospectus (owner's manual) for each fund you will be using at Vanguard or TIAA. Both mutual fund firms have licensed salaried representatives that provide accurate information about accounts and funds. Both offer low-cost index funds that hold a broad representation of the market returns of 10-12%. This is the building block to accumulating wealth.

Both firms are focused on you, not on profits.

Our strategy is to buy mutual funds with stocks of growing companies worldwide. No Wall Street guru can predict the future winners. Most can't do better than 50%—a flip of the coin. Your investments provide long-term growth of 10-12% annually on average with the benefit of avoiding single company or industry failures. It provides exposure to new growth potential around the world with less risk than holding one company, one sector, or one country. Some years our account is up 33% and some years down 22%. However, we double our money every 7-9 years *over time.*

It is the amount we KEEP that matters!

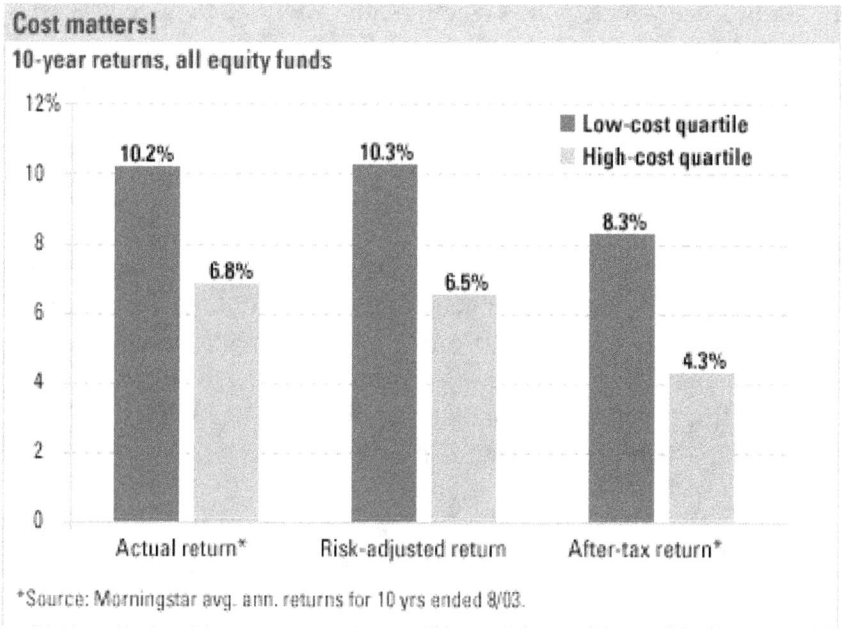

Invest every month automatically

We need to find at least $250 per month to invest in order to build our account. We can build wealth by following the strategy outlined in the previous chapters, but we need to have at least $250 available in the first place. In my experience, it doesn't matter how much people earn, most say they don't have the money to invest for their future. "Today is hard enough," they complain.

Yes, that may well be, but if we don't find the $250 we won't have a very happy tomorrow. We have to go back to our goal. We want to build wealth: accumulating $1,000,000 over time. Based on the way wealth compounds, we need to invest at least $250 a month, every month. We need to be consistent for the **miracle of compounding** to work. It is the habit that makes wealth.

A Spending Plan is a way to set priorities for our regular spending. We can accumulate $1 million to accomplish all that we want to do in life by using just 10 percent of our income to buy assets that "grow by themselves."

Using a Spending Plan is **like brushing your teeth**—it's a habit that isn't that difficult to learn—then it is automatic. Our Spending Plan must include what we need to function now and in the future. Like building a business, it takes planning and following the steps we talked about so far.

Some investors include the $250 in their automatic bill payment or have the trustee debit their account automatically. Others set up family goals and decide to put a certain amount in a separate account for each goal. In this way, they keep the wealth-building process in the forefront of their monthly bill payments.

Whatever way works for you. The important thing is to change the status of wealth-building from a vague future desire to a monthly habit. "Set it and forget it" is the theme of investing.

Most people find that the easiest way is to set up an automatic debit of their checking account by the trustee at the time of the application for the Roth IRA. If we are using a Roth 401k or an employer account, we set up the retirement account with automatic contributions. We are less likely to quit if a trustee debits monthly.

Some people are successful by making a written plan. They

have some idea of how much they will need at some time in the future. The account is set up as a Roth IRA so the ***contributions*** are not taxed when used before age 59.5. After that age, there are no taxes at all—EVER.

Another benefit of using a Spending Plan is that we become focused on how we spend our money. We are more inclined to buy only what we need. For financial services, I compiled the ***The Insiders Guides*** for each area—insurance, securities, etc. They provide an easy way to save $3,000 or more on financial products we already use. https://www.amazon.com/Insiders-Guides-Discount-Financial-Services/dp/143480593X

We can't build wealth by spending more than we earn. Building wealth takes patience and commitment to contributing to our 'investment business' every month. Some people don't try to be disciplined investors. They let the trustee debit the $250 or 10% every month so they can't fail to become a millionaire.

Are you paying too much?

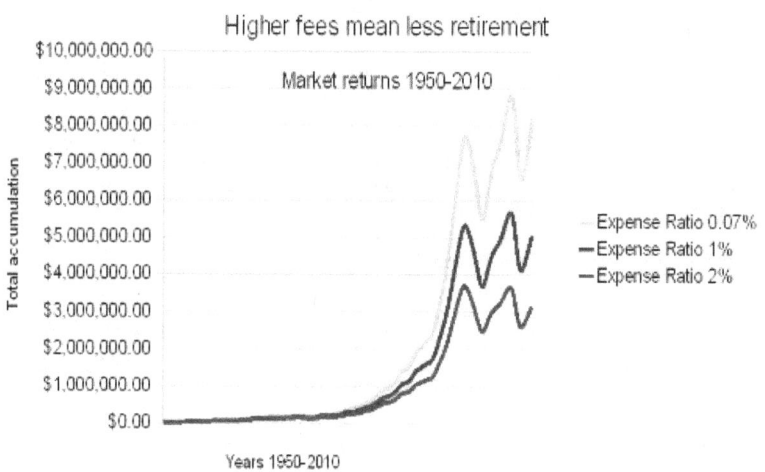

Buy low-cost financial products

It is easy to build wealth if we already have a pile of money. It takes 7-9 years to accumulate $1 million if you already have $500,000. Check the chart.

Monthly	Accumulation at 12% per year									
	5	10	15	20	25	30	35	40	45	50
$100	$8,167	$23,004	$49,958	$98,925	$187,884	$349,496	$643,095	$1,176,477	$2,145,469	$3,905,834
$200	$16,334	$46,008	$99,916	$197,850	$375,768	$698,992	$1,286,190	$2,352,954	$4,290,938	$7,811,668
$300	$24,501	$69,012	$149,874	$296,775	$563,652	$1,048,488	$1,929,285	$3,529,431	$6,436,408	$11,717,502
$500	$40,835	$115,020	$249,790	$494,625	$939,420	$1,747,480	$3,215,475	$5,882,385	$10,727,346	$19,529,169

But how do we capture that first $500,000, that first $250,000, or even that first $50,000? It comes from buying assets that 'grow by themselves.' It takes time and the easiest way to make sure we reach our goal is to **make our monthly contributions automatic**.

But where do we get the $250 a month? The best way is to "REDIRECT" the **cash we already spend** on things we really don't need or can buy for less. This is how millionaires stay millionaires. They don't over pay!

Most working people waste $3,000 or more each year on financial services. We must shop for financials like we shop for groceries: buy the house brand and use discounts. For instance, the difference between paying full price for a new car and a 3-year-old model can be 40% or more.

Let's take some examples of **annual savings**:

Auto insurance: save $400 or more EVERY year by changing/dropping some features we don't need. Drop towing/life insurance.

Home insurance: save $200 or more EVERY year by changing one limit--deductible. Claims are very infrequent.

Life insurance: save $1,000 or more EVERY year by using direct to consumer term insurer. SBLI.

Mutual funds: save $2-3,000 EVERY year by using low-cost providers. Low-cost beat high-cost every period.

Bank: save $120 EVERY year by using a low-cost provider of the benefits we usually use. Credit Union.

Mortgage: save $2,000 on closings and lower interest rates.

Investments: earn 15-30% a year guaranteed just by paying off credit cards.

Tax refund: Averages $3,022 so reduce withholdings W-4.

Using the ***The Insiders' Guides to Buying Discount Financial Services: Buy Direct and Save $3,000 Every Year,*** we can REDIRECT the $250 a month without having to give up anything. We don't need to tighten our belt or make a budget. We can give up things we would not benefit from anyway. Best example:

MetLife charged $983 for a $300,000 30-year **term policy**. This same $300,000 benefit was sold by Savings Bank Life Insurance for $384 a year. Their financial strength ratings are A+ and their underwriting requirements are the same. The difference, $599, over 30 years is $17,970. If invested, this difference can add $175,000 to OUR **account**.

This strategy—to cut out the middle people who are taking your money with little benefit to you—makes sense and works! But the most important part of our strategy is to keep investing: ***buying more shares of mutual funds when they are 'on sale.'***

They are on sale when the market FALLS. We do the opposite of what other people do because we want to have $1 million later.

2011 Total Return	Fund	Long-term Return*	Longevity
1.97%	500 Index	10.36%	since 1976
-1.74%	Energy	12.71%	since 1984
-3.73%	Extended Market	9.96%	since 1987
11.45%	Health	16.30%	since 1984
-13.68%	International Growth	10.50%	since 1981
-1.84%	PRIMECAP	12.79%	since 1984
-2.80%	Small Cap Index	10.26%	since 1960
9.63%	Wellesley Income	10.16%	since 1970
-4.00%	Windsor	11.00%	since 1958
2.70%	Windsor II	10.18%	since 1985
0.00%	Average	11.42%	

*Average Annual Returns as of 12/31/11.

We must ignore what others are doing when some markets fall because we are gaining more shares NOT cashing in at panic prices. We never sell in a panic falling market: we buy on sale.

Manage investments once a year

> "We continue to make more money when ***snoring*** than when active."
>
> Warren Buffett

This is the advice of the most successful investor of our day. He is making it clear that we should NOT touch our investments very often. We buy shares of the top companies and hold them all our lives—selling them only for our retirement income.

Wall Street makes money on transactions. We don't trade. We ignore the market and keep buying so we end up with $1 million. When the market is down we keep our mind on the chart on p. 17. We have to remember Warren Buffett's advice and hold on to stocks/stock funds. In fact, Mr Buffett says "**our favorite holding period is forever.**" http://www.berkshirehathaway.com/letters/1988.html

Even if the market drops; it will rise. It fell 22% in 2002 and rose 29% in 2003. We only have to look at our tax-FREE account once a year. We make sure we are making contributions to the specific mutual fund that is down for the year. We don't 'rebalance.'

When we first start investing, we use the STAR Index. After we had accumulated enough to buy the 500 Index ($3,000), we trade shares of the STAR Index for shares of the 500. We keep buying into the 500 Index until we have the minimum for the next one. We repeat this pattern until we have the minimum in each. Then we add to the one that is down for the year. Repeat each year.

As we accumulate the minimum for each fund, then transfer into the next one, we do not need to pay tax on the sale because we are using a tax-FREE Roth IRA. This is part of the **miracle of compounding**. After accumulating a large proportion of our goal, adding the $250 per month does not matter to the outcome. We can borrow to pay for cars, vacations, other goals. For instance, our client whose account is shown on page 12 took $25,000 for a used luxury car in the year the account hit over half a million. His account total did not suffer long term. He repaid at $250 a month.

Manage investments only once a year is wise advice. Our tax-FREE account does not require us to hire an advisor to manage it.

We have the ***power of compounding*** so we don't need advisors.

Plan spending wisely

We have used the 10 funds to build wealth. We have learned to be patient and accumulate $1,000,000 or more. We have paid back any amounts that we borrowed to pay cash for large purchases. We have been fortunate that the historical averages of market returns have produced the accumulations we set as our goals.

NOW WHAT?

Now we can take 8% out of the account each year and pay no income taxes. As of 2017, most states follow the IRS code on our **account**, a Roth IRA. https://www.irs.gov/retirement-plans/roth-iras

Many people move 60% of their money into a balanced fund like the Wellesley Income fund. It has produced over 9% per year on average since 1970. They created a retirement spending plan that assured them of that monthly income of a fixed dollar amount with this Guide. amazon.com/Your-Retirement-Spending-Plan-enough.

We have to create our $1,000,000 nest egg in order to provide the same buying power as we have today because of inflation. I am assuming that most working families will need at least $50,000 a year to live on in retirement. We don't know what will happen to Social Security by 2034. We don't know what employer pensions might look like by then. I am assuming that inflation will continue so planning is crucial to success in retirement.

Inflation, about 2.7%, will make the goods we buy now for $50,000 cost about $80,000. If Social Security or employer pensions can add to our basic income, that is fine. But we don't want to count on them. If there is a bad year like 2008, we are not taking money out of our growth funds at a bad time. The balanced fund has bonds which has traditionally been less volatile.

The funds we have listed above include some of the most consistent low volatility returns over time. Since our account is not taxable, there are no taxes when we take our monthly income later. We may not have to pay tax on our other income like Social Security and/or our qualified retirement funds. The gains on our account are tax-FREE after age 59.5. Unlike pensions and annuities, this account is tax-FREE.

We pay $99,000 $3,000 for 33 years and $901,000 is FREE of tax.

The Keys to Wealth

1. **Costs matter**: Broker/advisor cost 1% to 3% every year

   If you use a salesperson, costs take HALF your money!
   $3,000 per year @11%   for 33 years = $1,018,177
   $3,000 per year @11-1% for 33 years = $778,768
   $3,000 per year @11-2% for 33 years = $613,805
   $3,000 per year @11-3% for 33 years = $486,634
   www.moneychimp.com/calculator/compound_interest_calculator.htm

2. Broker/advisor stock-picking does not beat index funds over time. No money manager has been able to beat the markets consistently. No one can forecast the future. http://investa.com/man-vs-machine-the-great-stock-showdown-wall-street-journal-05-10-13/

3. **Compounding** creates investment success; NOT buying and selling. The chance of you doing both, at the right times, is near zero. Warren Buffett's holding period is "forever." No trading!

4. A **tax-FREE** investment account increases your balance 30%.

5. Putting all your money in one stock or market sector guarantees failure over time. No one investment is perfect. Buy a **group of growing global businesses in a low-cost fund.**

6. '**Dollar cost average**' buying technique lowers the cost of shares over time. When you invest a fixed amount each month, you buy more mutual fund shares when the price is low and less when high. Over time, you will own more shares at a lower average cost.

7. **Consistency** wins over the long term. Quick in and out trading only benefits Wall Street. Market timing may work for a short time but the odds of being right on the buy and sell are very long.

8. **Patience** is required to allow your money to work for you. Building a business takes time. Investing is *betting* to most of us.

Use the *Buffett Strategy* to reach your goals

Fidelity found that the ***most successful investors*** were those that forgot their account or died. Most wealthy investors have learned that patience is the Buffett secret to investing. They see how ***costs destroy*** their portfolio compounding. They avoid sales hype and use the strategy discussed above. That is why they stay rich.

Sometimes people need to confirm their decisions. Most fund companies have advisors on salary to confirm our decisions. The industry has made building wealth a mystery so it can take $1.3 Trillion from our accounts year after year. The average advisor-run account return was only 3.79%. The fees buy toys for the Pimps of Wall Street. Over time the costs compound and can take up to 63% of your total possible accumulations. Advisors like to buy and sell creating taxes and fees. Inflation took 2.7% of the 3.79%.

As Buffett said, **compounding is key** to reaching our money goals. If we pay 2% to get 10-12%, we net 8-10%. We know that no advisor can guarantee 10-12%. Advisors charge 1-3% whether they beat the averages or not. Advisors don't give refunds!

The clear winning strategy is to use the 10 funds and let compounding work its magic. Over time using a tax-FREE account with low fees, we can accumulate $1,000,000 from $250 a month at 10-12%. Using a compounding calculator moneychimp.com/calculator/compound_interest_calculator.htm, we find the range is 31 to 35 years. If our spouse has an account, we can shorten the time to 26-29 years for a family $1 million.

If we use an advisor, we may give up over $500,000 of $1 million in total accumulation. Research has shown that the average investor actually earns just 3.79% not 11% annually over time. Verify: moneychimp.com/features/market_cagr.htm

Our 10 funds for building wealth work because they are low-cost strategies inside a unique **tax-FREE trust account.** This eliminates the biggest killers of wealth: TAXES and FEES. We can be our own masters of tax-FREE wealth with patience. There is no need to pick stocks or hire expensive advisors or product pushers with hidden fees. We can do it ourselves as long as we have a plan. The plan is following Warren Buffett's strategy.

You must take the first step. Advisors can't profit from these steps. You have to call Vanguard or TIAA *yourself* to set up your account. Advisors can't. It takes about 1 hour to set up a Roth IRA for each of you. You can do it online or by phone. You can begin with TIAA and $100 automatic contributions or Vanguard with $1,000. Put the contributions on automatic so you don't have to decide every month whether to invest. That is usually how people fail. Life happens and there is always an emergency that requires cash. But future life happens too and you want to be spending your $80,000 a year not praying Washington won't cut Social Security benefits every year.

If you have been investing, you can convert portions of your IRA each year, paying tax on the earnings as you go. Over time, your Roth account will grow with earnings that are tax-FREE. This money may reduce your overall tax in retirement. It also is a great estate planning tool since no tax will be due from your heirs either.

There is a clear reason why "working millionaires" become wealthy. It is not luck or inheritance. Millions of immigrants to this country have done it before. They lived below their means. They saved and invested in businesses. They did not let temporary cash flow problems stop them from building wealth. They used the same path to building wealth every day.

As many clients say, "I never even miss the contributions because I never see them. Then all of a sudden, I see my statement has $25,000, $50,000, $250,000, $1,000,000, $2,000,000. We are talking real money here."

The real secret to investing is **compounding**. Buffett says:

"My wealth has come from a combination of living in America, some lucky genes, and **compound interest**."

Avoid Wall Street sales hype and keep ALL your earnings.

Pay $99,000 ($250 month, 33 years); Receive $1,000,000

Call Vanguard **800-551-8631** or TIAA **800-223-1200** today.

The Author

Law Steeple has been in financial services for over 20 years. He was a managing executive of the sales units of a number of bank securities firms. He is the author of Tax-FREE Wealth: How to use the tax laws for $2,000,000 free of tax. He is one of the insiders who contributed to the The Insiders Guides set of buyers' guides edited by Dan Keppel. The guides provide specific ways to save on all financial services. ***The Insiders' Guides to Buying Discount Financial Services: Buy Direct and Save $3,000 Every Year*** is available at Amazon, Barnes and Noble, Abebooks. Law lives in New Jersey and Florida.

See Law's author page:

https://www.amazon.com/Law-Steeple-MBA/e/B008BH2SKE

Follow Dan's blog: http://dankeppel.blogspot.com/

WHEN WILL YOU START YOUR TAX-FREE $1 MILLION ACCOUNT?

Start date for you --

Start date for your spouse---

Start date for you kids--

Start date for your in-laws--

Start date for your loved ones-------------------------------------

www.ingramcontent.com/pod-product-compliance
Lightning Source LLC
Chambersburg PA
CBHW050035230526
45470CB00003B/1299